A Guide for Using

Strega Nona

in the Classroom

Based on the tale retold and illustrated by Tomie dePaola

*This guide written by **Patsy Carey and Susan Kilpatrick***
Illustrated by Theresa M. Wright

Teacher Created Materials, Inc.
6421 Industry Way
Westminster, CA 92683
www.teachercreated.com
©1993 Teacher Created Materials, Inc.
Reprinted, 2003
Made in U.S.A.
ISBN 1-55734-436-1

Table of Contents

Introduction and Sample Lessons

A good book can touch the lives of children like a good friend. The pictures, words, and characters can inspire young minds as they turn to literary treasures for companionship, recreation, comfort, and guidance. Great care has been taken in selecting the books and unit activities that comprise the primary series of Literature Units. Teachers who use this literature unit to supplement their own valuable ideas can plan the activities using one of the following methods.

A Sample Lesson Plan

The sample lessons below provide the teacher with a specific set of lesson plan suggestions. Each of the lessons can take from one to several days to complete and can include all or some of the suggested activities. Refer to the "Suggestions for Using the Unit Activities" on pages 6 - 10 for information relating to the unit activities.

A Unit Planner

For the teacher who wishes to tailor the suggestions on pages 6 - 10 in a format other than that prescribed in the Sample Lesson Plan, a blank unit planner is provided on page 4. On a specific day you may choose the activities you wish to include by writing the activity number or a brief notation about the activity. Space has been provided for reminders, comments, and other pertinent information relating to each day's activities. Reproduce copies of the Unit Planner as needed.

Sample Lesson Plan

Lesson 1

- Introduce the book by using some or all of unit activities 1- 4 on page 6.
- Read "About the Author" with your students. (page 5)
- Discuss the new vocabulary with the students. (page 6)
- Discuss the "Big Ideas." (page 7)
- Prepare for reading the story by completing unit activities 7 and 8. (page 7)
- Read the story for enjoyment.

Lesson 2

- Read the story a second time.
- Prepare pocket charts and use the Bloom's Taxonomy cards and activities to involve students in critical thinking. (pages 11 -14)
- Use the "Story Summary Sentence Strips." (pages 15-16)
- Recite "Strega Nona's Magic Pot." (page 17)

Lesson 3

- Construct and write about scenes from *Strega Nona*. (pages 23 - 24)
- Sequence story events. (pages 25 - 27)
- Practice map skills. (pages 37 - 38)
- Analyze characters. (page 28)
- Begin practicing Reader's Theater script. (pages 45 47)

Lesson 4

- Practice punctuation with "Who Said It?" (pages 29 - 30)
- Follow directions to complete a picture. (page 40)
- Learn a song about Strega Nona and Big Anthony. (pages 43 - 44)
- Help students distinguish between real and make-believe. (pages 33 - 34)
- Involve students with drama using stick puppets. (pages 18 - 22)
- Practice Reader's Theater script. (pages 45 - 47)

Lesson 5

- Design an apron for Strega Nona. (activity 22, page 9)
- Compare Strega Nona and Big Anthony. (page 32)
- Display and practice Strega Nona's chants. (page 31)
- Create crystal gardens. (page 39)
- Practice Reader's Theater script. (pages 45-47)

Lesson 6

- Write stories on pot shapes. (activity 26, page 10)
- Prepare graphs and practice counting and sorting skills. (pages 35 - 36)
- Make clay pots. (page 41)
- Prepare recipes on page 42. Serve foods after Reader's Theater presentation.
- Present Reader's Theater as a culminating activity. See page 10 for suggestions.

Unit Planner

Unit Activities

Date: _____

Notes/Comments

Unit Activities

Date: _____

Notes/Comments

Unit Activities

Date: _____

Notes/Comments

Unit Activities

Date: _____

Notes/Comments

Unit Activities

Date: _____

Notes/Comments

Unit Activities

Date: _____

Notes/Comments

Getting to Know the Book and Author

About the Book

(*Strega Nona* is published in the U.S. by Simon & Schuster Inc. It is also available in Canada from Simon & Schuster, in the United Kingdom from International Book Dist., and in Australia from Prentice Hall.)

Big Anthony answers Strega Nona's ad and is hired to weed the garden, feed the goats, and fetch the water. Strega Nona asks Big Anthony not to touch her valuable pasta pot, but Big Anthony doesn't listen.

Big Anthony sees the pot bubbling over with pasta after Strega Nona recites a magic chant. He brags to the townspeople that he, too, can magically produce enough pasta to feed them all. However, Big Anthony missed an important detail while eavesdropping on Strega Nona, and he can't get the pot to stop cooking pasta!

The pasta threatens to overrun the town and nothing seems to be able to save the town from disaster. Fortunately, Strega Nona returns just in time to recite the chant and blow the three kisses that will make the pot stop. Big Anthony learns his lesson the hard way when he has to eat the pasta all by himself.

About the Author

Tomie dePaola was born in Meriden, Connecticut, in 1934, and graduated from the Pratt Institute in 1956. He has earned advanced degrees since that time. Besides illustrating and writing children's books, he is an artist and has been a costume and set designer. He also taught art and theater in various New England colleges. In 1976, *Strega Nona* was named a Caldecott Honor Book. He currently lives in Wilmot Flat, New Hampshire.

Tomie dePaola's family and heritage influenced him in such a way that he developed an interest in old stories or folktales about Italy.

Stories and recollections from friends and family are the basis of many of Tomie dePaola's books. He uses humor to develop his characters and plots, and beautifully illustrates his own books.

Suggestions for Using the Unit Activities

Use some or all of the following suggestions to introduce students to *Strega Nona* and to extend their appreciation of the book through activities that cross the curriculum.

1. Use *Strega Nona* along with other old stories to comprise a unit on folktales. With *Strega Nona*, the following themes can be explored:

   • assuming responsibility for one's actions

   • the effects of eavesdropping, bragging, and teasing

   • the importance of completing chores

2. Before you begin the unit, prepare the vocabulary cards, story question hats, and sentence strips for the pocket chart activities. (See samples, patterns, and directions on pages 11-16.)

3. Engage prior knowledge and oral language skills by asking the children to identify or recall any Italian foods they have recently eaten. Show pictures of pizza, spaghetti, and a variety of Italian foods from magazines or a nutrition unit.

4. Ask if anyone knows where Italy is located on a map. On which continent is Italy located? Help students find Italy on a map and a globe. Locate Calabria in the southern part of Italy. Compare the size of Italy to the state in which the students live.

   If the class has studied about Columbus, ask if anyone remembers an explorer who was born in Italy. Locate Genoa on a map.

5. Discuss the meaning of the following words in context before reading the story. Make several copies of the pot pattern on page 13. Write the words below on the pots. Display the pasta pots on a pocket chart. (See page 11 for directions on making a pocket chart.)

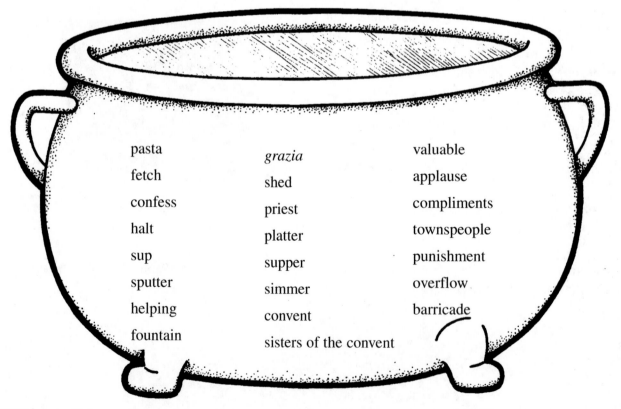

pasta	*grazia*	valuable
fetch	shed	applause
confess	priest	compliments
halt	platter	townspeople
sup	supper	punishment
sputter	simmer	overflow
helping	convent	barricade
fountain	sisters of the convent	

Suggestions for Using the Unit Activities *(cont.)*

6. Provide exposure to the following "Big Ideas:"

   Discuss the concept of responsibility:

   - Is it a good idea to eavesdrop on other people's conversations?

   - Should we use other people's belongings without their permission?

   Talk about the changes in food after cooking:

   - How does pasta change after being placed in boiling water?

   - What changes have you seen in popcorn, ice cream, butter, gelatin, and meat as they are prepared for eating?

   Remind children of the basic food groups. In which group does pasta belong? (Bread, Cereal, Rice, and Pasta Group)

7. Display the cover of *Strega Nona*. Have the children look for any clues that might convey the story setting.

8. Ask the students to make a prediction about what Strega Nona will do with the cooking pot. Ask: Does the story take place now or long ago? Read the story aloud to discover what happens in the little town of Calabria.

9. Develop critical thinking skills with the story questions on page 14. The questions are based on Bloom's Taxonomy and are provided in each of Bloom's Level's of Learning. Make hats using these story questions. Refer to page 12 for information on how to make the story question hats and suggestions on how to use the story questions.

10. Refer to the sentences on pages 15-16 to prepare Story Summary Sentence Strips. Cut out the sentence strips. Laminate a set of sentences for use with a pocket chart. Work with students on some or all of the following activities.

    - On the pocket chart, sequence the sentences in the order in which the events happened in the story.

    - Use the sentences to retell the story.

    - Divide the class into small groups and distribute a few sentence strips to each group. Ask the groups to act out the part of the story represented by the sentence.

    In addition to these activities, you may wish to reproduce the pages and have students read the sentences aloud to a partner or take them home to read to a parent, sibling, etc.

11. Reproduce "Strega Nona's Magic Pot" (page 17). Divide the class into four groups and assign each group a verse of the poem. Have the groups choral read and act out their verses. As an extension, have children recite Shel Silverstein's "Spaghetti" from *Where the Sidewalk Ends* (HarperCollins Child Books, 1974).

Suggestions for Using the Unit Activities *(cont.)*

12. Prepare Stick Puppet Theaters following the suggestions and directions on page 18. Allow the students to construct puppets by coloring, cutting, and gluing puppets on tongue depressors. Use the suggestions for stick puppets found on page 19.

13. Have students construct a scene from *Strega Nona* and write about some of the events in the story. Directions, patterns, and sentence blocks are provided on pages 23-24.

14. Sharpen students' map skills by having them use the map of Italy on page 37 and answer the questions on page 38.

15. Provide practice in sorting, counting, graphing, and making comparisons by making pasta graphs. Give each child a copy of the graph on page 35 and a resealable plastic bag containing four different kinds of pasta: shells, elbow macaroni, spirals, and rigatoni. Each bag should contain no more than 8 pieces of each kind of pasta; provide an assorted number of each pasta. Instruct students to sort and graph the pieces of pasta in their bags. You might want students to glue the pasta to the paper graph or you can have them color the graph and save the pasta to use again. Distribute copies of page 36. Have students complete the graphs, record the information, and share their results.

16. Help students learn to sequence important story events with the activity on pages 25-27. This can be done as a whole-class activity or students can work in cooperative pairs or groups.

17. Use "Character Clouds" on page 28 to help students choose important facts, details, or traits about some of the characters in *Strega Nona*. This activity may be presented as a whole-class or cooperative group activity.

18. Students can practice the use of quotation marks and other forms of punctuation with "Who Said It?" on pages 29-30.

19. Help students learn and write Strega Nona's magic chants and illustrate them with a black pot, real pasta, and three kisses! On the chalkboard or a large chart, write Strega Nona's songs (chants) to start and stop the magic pot. In the appropriate boxes on page 31, have children copy Strega Nona's chants to make pasta in the magic pot. For younger children, you may wish to fill in the chants on page 31 before copying the page. Reproduce the pot on page 13 on black construction paper. (Enlarge the pattern if desired.) Follow the directions on page 31 for assembling the chants and the magic pot.

Suggestion's for Using the Unit Activities *(cont.)*

20. Use a Venn diagram to compare Strega Nona and Big Anthony. Have students complete "Alike and Different" on page 32 by writing in the appropriate areas how the two characters are alike and how they are different. This activity may be presented to the whole class, or you may wish to have the class work in small groups and share their ideas when they are done. A sample Venn diagram is provided on the right.

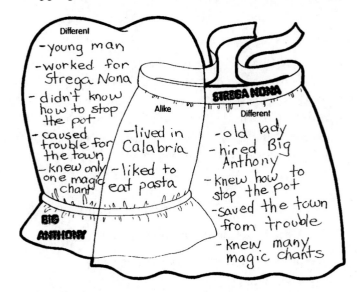

21. Help students distinguish between real and make-believe situations. Provide each student with two 3" x 5" (8 cm x 13 cm) index cards, one with the word "real" written on it, and the other labeled with the words "make-believe." If possible, use two different colors of index cards and laminate them for durability. Read several statements, some real and some make-believe, and ask children to hold up the appropriate card after each statement is read.

    Reproduce pages 33 and 34. Have students complete the "Real or Make-Believe?" activity by cutting out the sentence boxes on page 33 and pasting each box under the correct heading on page 34.

22. Have students design a new apron for Strega Nona. Provide each student with a 9" x 12" (23 cm x 30 cm) piece of white construction paper. Lay the paper horizontally on a desk and fold the top down about 1½" (3 cm). This becomes the waist band of the apron. Attach a length of ribbon to each end of the waistband.

    Work with children to compose short sentences about the most important events in *Strega Nona*. Have them write the sentences on the waistband. Children can glue sequins, buttons, colorful fabric scraps, yarn, etc., to the rest of the apron. String the aprons together by tying the ribbons and display the aprons across a wall.

23. Involve the students in designing their own clay pots. Directions for making clay pots are provided on page 41. As an extension, have children fill their "magic pots" with uncooked macaroni and tell or write a story about their "magic macaroni pots."

Suggestions for Using the Unit Activities *(cont.)*

24. Students can discover the "magic" of making things grow as Strega Nona did by creating crystal gardens. See page 39 for directions and a list of materials.

25. Use the "What's Cooking?" activities on page 42 to prepare some Pasta Quickies and Witch's Brew.

26. Reproduce the pot pattern on page 13. You may enlarge the pattern if desired. Copy the writing ideas below on a chart or the chalkboard. Have each student choose a topic from the list and write about it on lined paper, sized to fit inside the pot shape. Cut out and glue the students' writings in the pots. Cut out the pots and display them on a bulletin board. Or, make a shape book by cutting two pot shapes from black construction paper (for front and back covers) and attaching the students' stories between the covers.

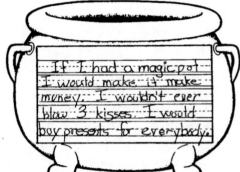

Writing Ideas:

- I know how to cook pasta. Here are the steps.

- Strega Nona was a good citizen in Calabria.

- Following directions is important.

- If I had a magic pot, I would do several things.

27. Culminating Activity

Use the Reader's Theater script to involve the students in a dramatic interpretation of the book. Allow the students to discuss the following questions:

- What did Dominic do that he should not have done?

- How do you think Dominic felt when everyone was making fun of him? How do you feel when someone makes fun of you? What can you do when this happens?

- Is it a good idea to brag about yourself? What is the difference between bragging and telling some of your friends about something you're proud of?

Following the Reader's Theater script, sing "Strega Nona and Big Anthony" (pages 43-44) or "On Top of Spaghetti," which can be found in *Everybody Sings* by Debbie Coyle, DMC Publications, 2113 Creekwood Dr., Fort Collins, Colorado 80525.

Prepare for and practice the script several times before the end of the unit. You may wish to reproduce the invitation on page 48 and invite other classes and parents to see the play and enjoy the music. Display related projects. This would also be a good time to serve some of the pasta dishes and the beverage described on page 42.

Pocket Chart Activities

A pocket chart can be used to hold the vocabulary cards (page 6, activity 5), the story questions on hats (page 14), and the sentence strips (pages 15-16).

How to Make a Pocket Chart

If a commercial pocket chart is unavailable, you can make a pocket chart if you have access to a laminator. Begin by laminating a 24" x 36" (60 cm x 90 cm) piece of colored tagboard. Run about 20" (50 cm) of additional plastic. To make nine pockets, cut the clear plastic into nine equal strips. Space the strips equally down the 36" (90 cm) length of the tagboard. Attach each strip with cellophane tape along the bottom and sides. This will hold sentence strips, word cards, etc., and can be displayed in a learning center or mounted on a chalk tray for use with a group. When your pocket chart is ready, use it to display the sentence strips, vocabulary words, and question cards. A sample chart is provided below.

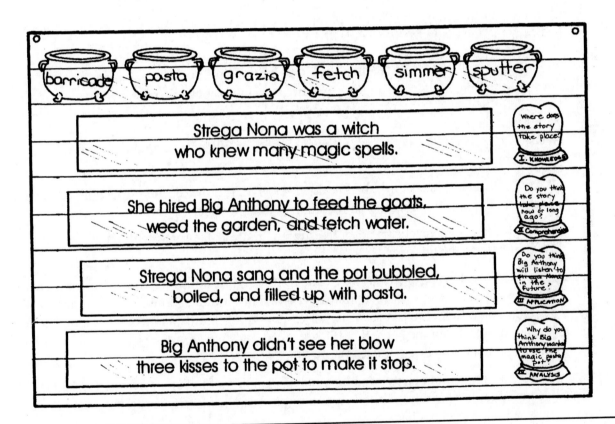

How to Use the Pocket Chart I

---

1. Make vocabulary cards by reproducing Strega Nona's pot pattern (page 13) on light blue or gray construction paper. Write vocabulary words on the pots. (See the vocabulary list on page 6.) Use the pot-shaped vocabulary cards to familiarize the children with difficult words and their meanings by giving them context clues.

   The pot pattern can also be enlarged and used to make student awards titled "Amazing Author" or "Wonderful Worker."

Pocket Chart Activities *(cont.)*

2. Reproduce several copies of the hat pattern (page 13) on six different colors of construction paper. Use one color of paper to represent each of Bloom's Levels of Learning.

For example:

   I. Knowledge (green)

   II. Comprehension (pink)

   III. Application (lavender)

   IV. Analysis (orange)

   V. Synthesis (blue)

   VI. Evaluation (yellow)

Write a question from page 14 on the appropriate color-coded hat. Write the level of the question on the brim. Laminate the hat for durability.

After reading *Strega Nona*, provide opportunities for the children to develop and practice higher level critical-thinking skills by using the questions on the color-coded hats with some or all of the following activities:

- Use a specified color-coded set of hats to question students at a particular Level of Learning.

- Have a child choose a card, read it aloud, or give it to the teacher to read aloud. The child answers the question or calls on a volunteer to answer it.

- Pair children. The teacher reads a question. Children take turns with their partners responding to the question.

- Play a game. Divide the class into teams. Ask for a response to a question from one of the question cards. Teams score a point for each appropriate response. If question cards have been prepared for several different stories, mix up the cards and ask team members to respond by naming the story that relates to the question. Extra points can be awarded if a team member answers the question as well.

3. Use sentence strips to practice oral reading and sequencing of the story events. Reproduce pages 15-16. If possible, laminate for durability. Cut out the sentence strips or prepare sentences of your own to use with the pocket chart.

Strega Nona was an old woman who knew many magic spells.

The townspeople tried to make a barricade. That didn't work!

Big Anthony didn't see her blow three kisses to the pot to make it stop.

Pocket Chart Patterns

See pages 11 and 12 for directions.

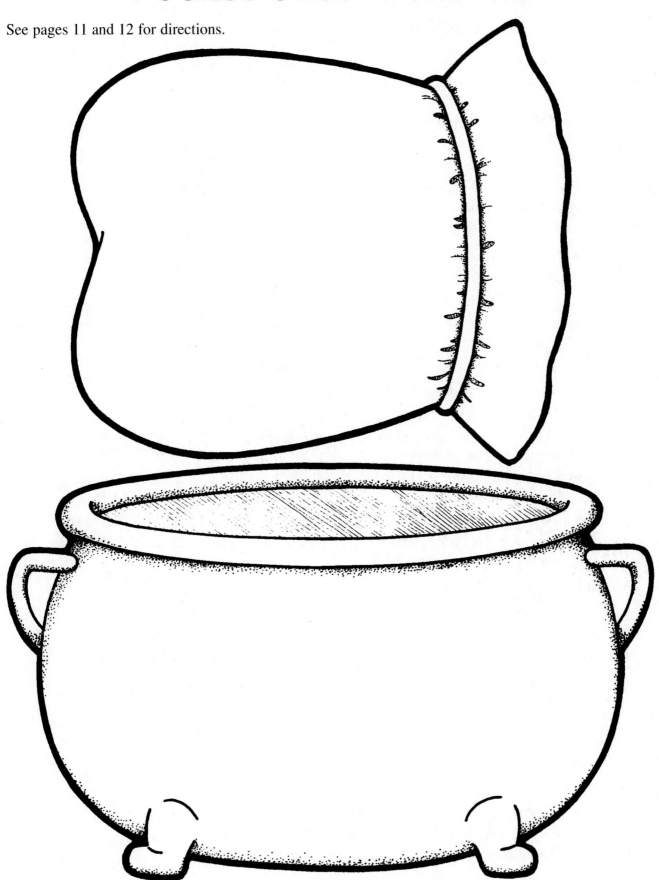

Story Questions

The following questions are based on Bloom's Levels of Learning.

Prepare the hats as directed on page 12. Write a different question from the Levels of Learning on each of the hats. Use the hats with the suggested activities in the unit.

I. Knowledge (ability to recall learned information)

- Name some of the ways Strega Nona used magic to help the townspeople.
- Why did Strega Nona put up a sign in the town square?
- Name some of Big Anthony's chores.
- Where does the story take place?
- What did the townspeople do to try to save the town from the pasta?

II. Comprehension (basic understanding of information)

- Do you think the story takes place now or long ago?
- Do you think it's a good idea to eavesdrop when other people are talking?
- What do you think would have happened to Big Anthony if Strega Nona hadn't arrived just in time?
- Can you think of any other stories about food causing problems?

III. Application (ability to do something new with information)

- Do you think Big Anthony will listen to Strega Nona in the future?
- How did Big Anthony feel when the townspeople laughed at him? How do you feel when someone laughs at you?
- Predict what would have happened if Big Anthony had seen Strega Nona blow three kisses at the pot.
- Do you think Strega Nona will trust Big Anthony the next time she leaves town?
- Have you ever done something you were told not to do? When have you had to be punished for your actions?

IV. Analysis (ability to examine the parts of a whole)

- Why do you think Big Anthony wanted to make pasta for the townspeople?
- Why do you think Big Anthony wanted to use the magic pasta pot?

V. Synthesis (ability to bring together information to make something new)

- Do you think Strega Nona had a good punishment for Big Anthony? Can you think of any other ways she might have punished Big Anthony?
- Would the story have been different if the magic pot had made chocolate instead of pasta? Tell how.

VI. Evaluation (ability to form and defend an opinion)

- Do you think Big Anthony learned his lesson? Why or why not?
- Big Anthony was called a liar and the townspeople wanted to punish him. What do you think of the way Big Anthony was treated?
- Would you recommend this story to a friend? Why or why not?

Story Summary Sentence Strips

See page 7 (activity 10) for directions.

Strega Nona was an old woman who knew many magic spells.

She hired Big Anthony to feed the goats, weed the garden, and fetch water.

Strega Nona said, "Don't ever touch the valuable pasta pot."

Stega Nona sang and the pot bubbled, boiled, and filled up with pasta.

Big Anthony didn't see her blow three kisses to the pot to make it stop.

Story Summary Sentence Strips *(cont.)*

See page 7 (activity 10) for directions.

Big Anthony sang to the pot.
It started to make pasta.

The townspeople used plates and forks to
eat the pasta. Soon it began to overflow.

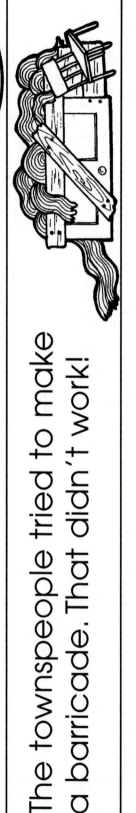

The townspeople tried to make
a barricade. That didn't work!

Strega Nona came back just in time. She knew
how to make the pot stop cooking pasta.

Big Anthony had to eat all the pasta!
The punishment fit the crime.

Strega Nona's Magic Pot

Strega Nona's magic pot
Cooked her pasta nice and hot,
Special words and kisses three,
Stopped the pot so magically.

Big Anthony thought he'd do the same;
He said the words, the pasta came.
But when he tried to stop the pot,
More pasta bubbled nice and hot.

The people yelled and ran around,
"There's too much pasta in our town!
Who can stop the magic pot
From making pasta nice and hot?"

Strega Nona as you knew,
Figured out just what to do.
Big Anthony, it now is time
To let the punishment fit the crime.

By Susan Kilpatrick

Stick Puppet Theaters

Make a class set of puppet theaters (one for each child), or make one theater for every 2-4 children. Stick puppet patterns and directions for making stick puppets are provided on pages 20-22.

Materials:

22" x 28" (56 cm x 71 cm) pieces of colored poster board
   (enough for each student or group of students)
markers, crayons, or paints
scissors or craft knife

Directions:

1. Fold the poster board 8" (20 cm) in from each of the shorter sides. (See picture below.)

2. Cut a "window" in the front panel large enough to accommodate two or three stick puppets.

3. Let the children personalize and decorate their own theaters.

4. Laminate the stick puppet theaters to make them more durable. You may wish to send the theaters home at the end of the year or save them to use year after year.

Stick Puppet Theaters *(cont.)*

Consider the following suggestions for using the puppets and puppet theaters:

- Prepare the stick puppets using the directions on page 20. Use the puppets and the puppet theaters with the Reader's Theater script on pages 45-47. (Let small groups of children take turns reading the parts and using the stick puppets.)

- Let children experiment with the puppets by telling the story in their own words or reading from the book.

- As you make statements about the characters in the book, children can hold up the correct stick puppet. Read each statement below and have students hold up the stick puppet that represents who or what might have said it.

"I start to bubble and boil when I hear the magic chant." (pasta pot)

"I forgot to blow 3 kisses." (Big Anthony)

"I went to visit my friend, Strega Amelia." (Strega Nona)

"I kept making pasta when someone forgot to blow 3 kisses." (pasta pot)

"I told everyone to get mattresses and tables to make a barricade to stop the pasta." (Mayor)

"I said, 'Let the punishment fit the crime.' " (Strega Nona)

"We laughed at Big Anthony." (Townspeople)

"I promise not to touch the pasta pot." (Big Anthony)

"You had better confess to the priest, Big Anthony. Such a lie!" (Sister of the Convent)

"We are lost! The pasta will cover our town!" (Townspeople)

Stick Puppet Patterns

Directions: Reproduce the patterns on index paper or construction paper. color the patterns. Cut along the dashed lines. To complete the stick puppets, glue each pattern to a tongue depressor. Use stick puppets with puppet theaters and/or the Reader's Theater script.

Make a second copy of the patterns to be used with the "Story Scenes form *Strega Nona*" activity described on page 23.

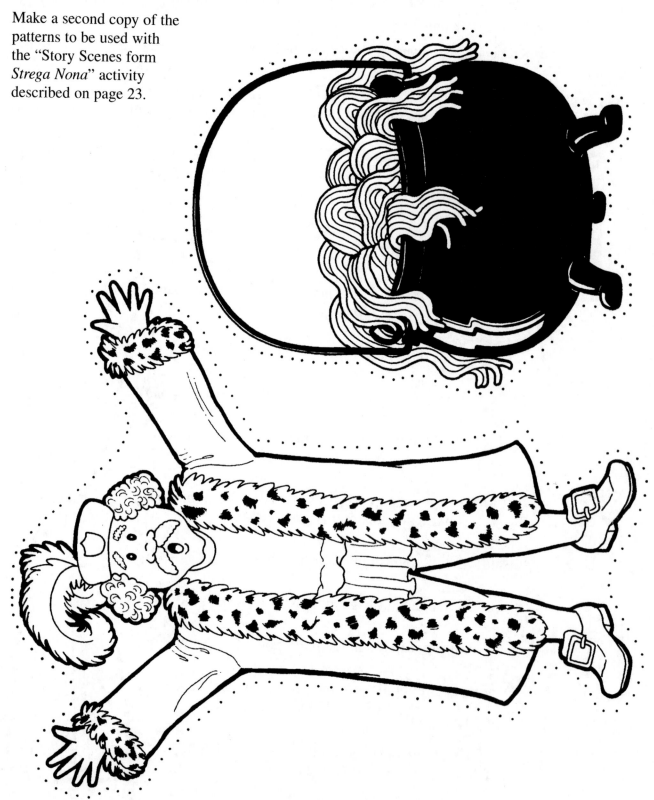

Stick Puppet Patterns *(cont.)*

See directions on page 20.

Stick Puppet Patterns *(cont.)*

See directions on page 20.

Story Scenes from *Strega Nona*

Directions:

Give each child a large sheet of white construction paper or butcher paper.

Have children draw Strega Nona's house and the pasta pot, as shown in the illustration to the right. You may wish to draw these on the chalkboard and have the children copy them on their papers.

Reproduce the figures of Big Anthony and Strega Nona on page 21. Color, cut out, and glue the figures to their pictures.

Reproduce and hand out a copy of the "Sentence Blocks" on page 24 to each student. Help students use the listed words at the top in sentences that relate the block title to the story. If age appropriate, reinforce the use of capitals, periods, quotations, commas in a series, contractions, possessives, etc.

Have the children cut out and glue the sentence blocks to their pictures. It is not necessary to place the sentence blocks in a specific order.

A set of sentence blocks might look like this:

1. Calabria	2. Strega Nona
Strega Nona lived in a house in Calabria, Italy.	"Strega Nona means "Grandma Witch."

3. Pot	4. Big Anthony
The pot bubbled, boiled and filled up with pasta.	Big Anthony couldn't stop the magic pot.

5. Pasta	6. Kisses
The pasta almost covered the town.	Strega Nona blew three kisses to the pot.

7. Punishment

Anthony's punishment was to eat up all the pasta!

Sentence Blocks

Directions: Use with the "Story Scenes from *Strega Nona*" activity on page 23.

1. Calabria

2. Strega Nona

3. Pot

4. Big Anthony

5. Pasta

6. Kisses

7. Punishment

Which Came First?

Directions: Have students color and cut out the peacock pattern below. Glue the pattern on a large piece of construction paper. Cut out the peacock feathers on pages 26-27. Each sentence tells about a different part of the story. Have students read and sequence the sentences. Ask them to write the numbers 1 through 6 in the circles at the top of the feathers to show the correct order of the sentences and glue the feathers in number order to the peacock.

Which Came First? *(cont.)*

See page 25 for directions.

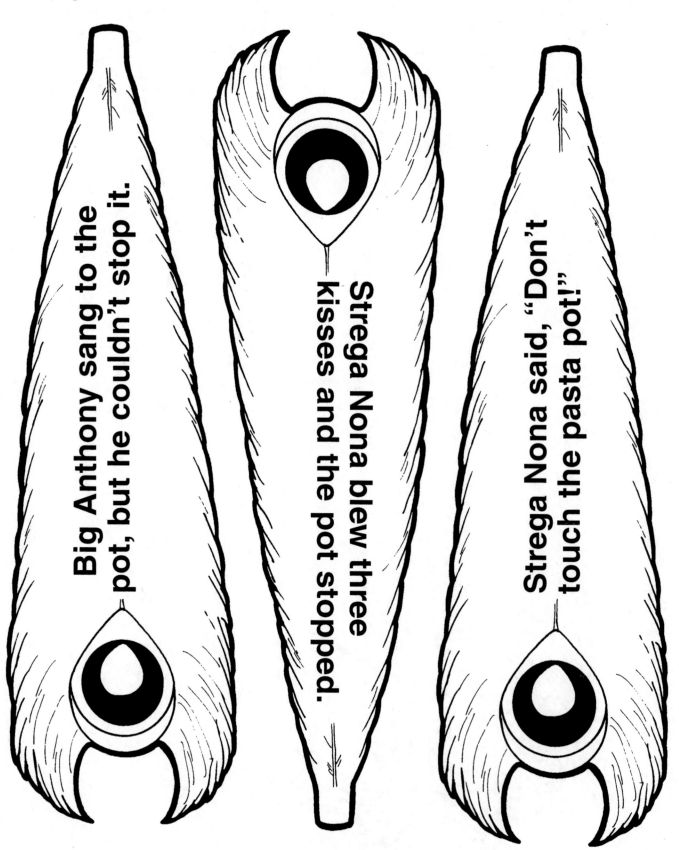

Big Anthony sang to the pot, but he couldn't stop it.

Strega Nona blew three kisses and the pot stopped.

Strega Nona said, "Don't touch the pasta pot!"

Which Came First? *(cont.)*

See page 25 for directions.

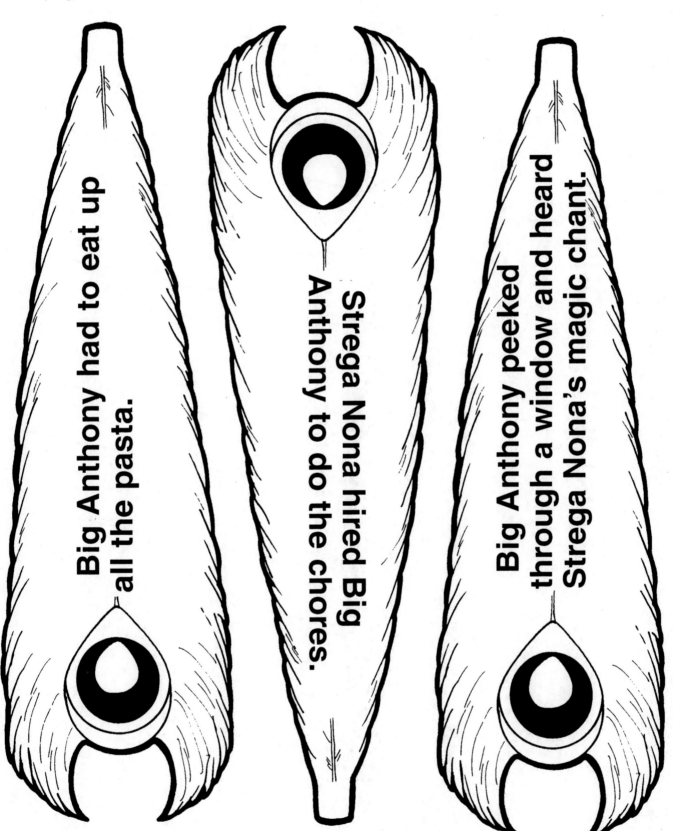

Big Anthony had to eat up all the pasta.

Strega Nona hired Big Anthony to do the chores.

Big Anthony peeked through a window and heard Strega Nona's magic chant.

Character Clouds

Name _____

Title of Book: _____

Author: _____

Who Said It?

Consider these suggestions for using page 30.

1. Reproduce and distribute page 30 to teams of two students.

2. Read and discuss the directions on the student page. You may wish to model the sample below with the class.

3. Have student teams share their characters and sentences with the class. As students read the quotations, encourage them to read with expression.

4. As an extension, let students make up sentences that might have been spoken by the three characters. Introduce or reinforce the use of quotation marks to indicate the characters' spoken words. Point out that when you use a speech bubble to show what a character says, quotation marks are not necessary. Have students write their hypothetical sentences and practice the use of quotation marks with them.

Sample

Name_____

Who Said It? *(cont.)*

Directions: Choose three characters from the story. Draw a different character in each box. Write his or her name on the line inside the box. Find an interesting, amusing, important, or funny sentence that was spoken by each of the three characters. Write the spoken words of the character in the bubble next to the character.

Name_____

A'Chanting We Will Go

Directions: Copy Strega Nona's chants in the boxes below. Cut out the boxes and glue them to a large piece of construction paper. Cut out the pot on page 13 and glue it on the construction paper. Then, glue pieces of uncooked pasta in and around the pasta pot. Read the chants to a classmate or family member.

CHANT TO START

_____

_____

_____

_____

CHANT TO STOP

_____

_____

_____

_____

**DON'T FORGET TO**

_____   _____   _____

Name_____

Alike and Different

Directions: In the pictures, write your ideas of how Strega Nona and Big Anthony are alike and how they are different.

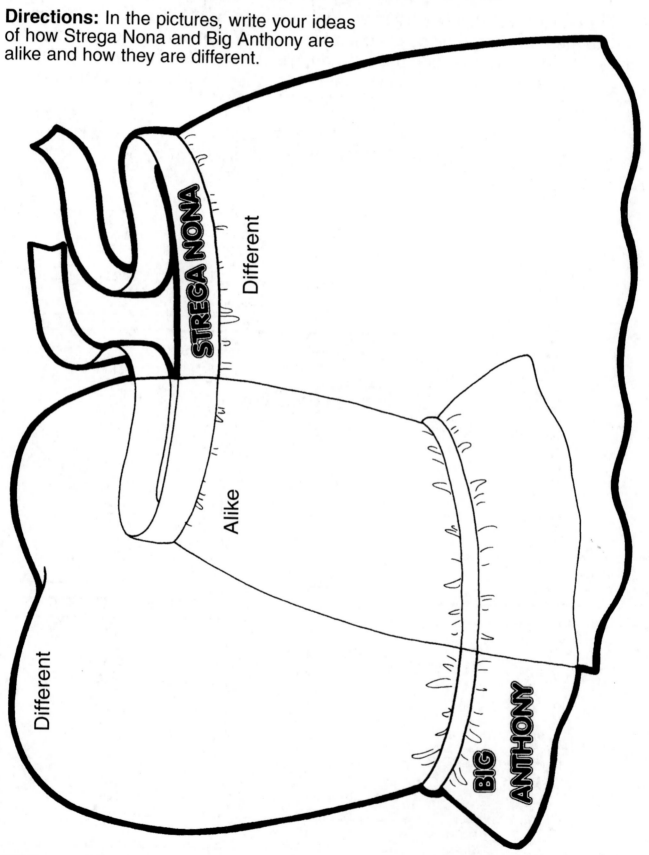

STREGA NONA

Different

Alike

Different

BIG ANTHONY

Name _____

Real or Make-Believe?

Directions: Read the sentences in the boxes below. Cut the boxes out. Glue each box under the correct heading on page 34.

Pasta is cooked in boiling water.	You can cook pasta by singing a chant.	You can eat pasta for dinner.
You can ask a grownup for help.	Doing something wrong can get you in trouble.	You can wave a magic wand to cast a spell.
		You could eat as much pasta as Big Anthony did.
Strega Nona can make magic potions.	You can visit a friend.	You can sweep the floor and wash dishes.
		Pasta can cover up a whole town.
		Blowing three kisses will make pasta stop cooking.

Name _____

Real or Make-Believe? *(cont.)*

Use with page 33.

Make-Believe

Real

Name_____

My Pasta Graph

Number of Pieces				
7				
6				
5				
4				
3				
2				
1				
0	shells	elbow macaroni	spirals	rigatoni

Kinds of Pasta

Pasta Graph Recording Sheet

Directions: Use the information from your graph to fill in the blanks below.

Recording Information

My pasta graph has:

_____ shells

_____ elbow macaroni

_____ spirals

_____ rigatoni

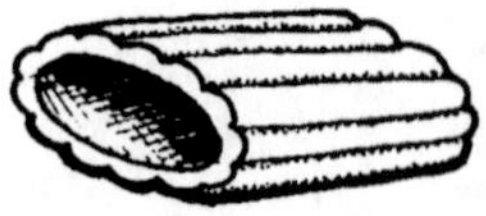

Checking for Understanding

I made these discoveries:

My graph has more _____

    than any other kind of pasta.

My graph has fewer _____

    than any other kind of pasta.

My friend's graph has more _____

    than any other kind of pasta.

I would like to eat _____

    more than any other kind of pasta.

36

Name_____

Mapping It Out

Directions: Use the map on this page to complete the activities on page 38.

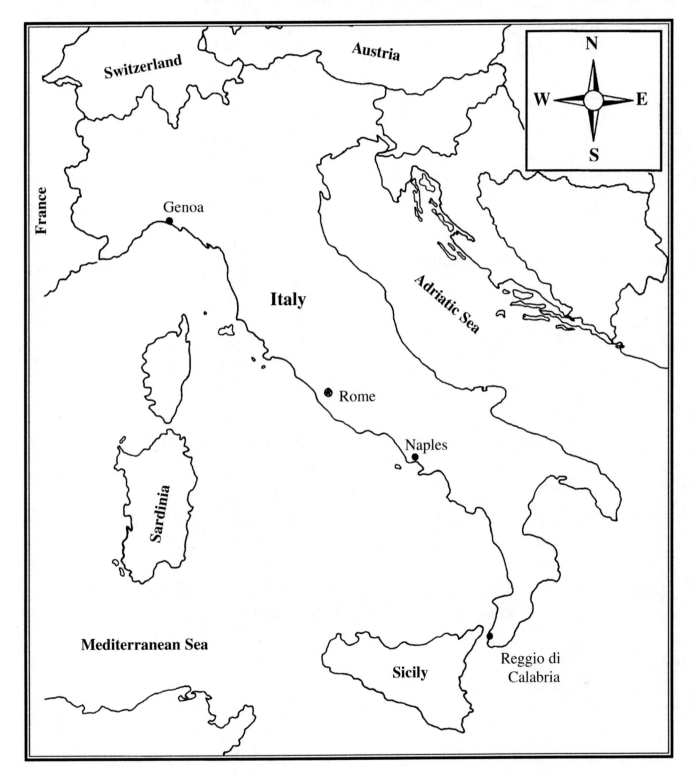

Name_____

Mapping It Out *(cont.)*

Directions: Use the map of Italy on page 37 to find the information below.

1. What is the capital of Italy? _____

2. Two islands shown on the map are _____
   and _____.

3. Is Calabria in the northern part of Italy or in the southern part of Italy?

   _____.

4. The names of two seas on the map are _____
   and _____.

5. Italy is shaped like a _____.

6. Christopher Columbus lived in Genoa. Circle it on the map.

7. Is Genoa in the northern part of Italy or in the southern part?

   _____

8. Two countries which border on Italy are _____
   and _____.

9. Find Italy on a world map and on a globe. Compare its size to that of the United States. Is Italy larger or smaller than the United States?

   _____

10. Draw a compass here:

Crystal Magic

Strega Nona used her magic to create many exciting and magical things. When your students make these beautiful crystal gardens, the results will seem like magic! You can explain that the mixture poured over the charcoal causes a chemical reaction which allows the crystals to grow.

Materials:

charcoal briquettes   *salt*

laundry bluing   *ammonia*

coffee can   *measuring spoons*

food coloring (a variety of colors)   *water*

aluminum pie tins, or foil-lined cardboard bowls

Mix the following solution in advance:

6 tablespoons (90 mL) salt

6 tablespoons (90 mL) laundry bluing

6 tablespoons (90 mL) water

3 tablespoons (45 mL) ammonia

Directions:

1. Provide the children with individual pie tins or cardboard bowls lined with foil. (Foil or tin helps to protect the top of the table.) Place one charcoal briquette into each bowl.

2. Have children squirt food coloring on the briquette. You may wish to have each child add two or three colors to sections of the briquette or give each child a specific color. Students can experiment with colors first by mixing the basic primary colors to make secondary colors. (The food coloring will be absorbed into the porous charcoal.)

3. Spoon the solution of salt, laundry bluing, water, and ammonia over the briquette every day for about two weeks.

4. Add more food coloring every two days. Note: Because the crystals are fragile and powdery, instruct the students not to disturb their gardens.

Name_____

Finish the Picture

Follow the directions below to finish the picture on this page.

1. Color Big Anthony's hat brown. Make his pants blue.

2. Color Strega Nona's skirt red.

3. Draw a bird in the window.

4. Show some spaghetti coming out of the pot. Color the pot black.

5. Draw a candle and a vase of flowers on the shelf.

6. Draw a rabbit by Big Anthony.

Pottery Fun

Strega Nona's magic pot was made of clay. Use the following materials and directions to make clay pots with your students.

Materials:

round margarine container or coffee can lid

ceramic clay (available at art supply stores and ceramic shops)

plastic covering for the work surface

craft stick, plastic fork, or knife

bowl of water

sponge

Directions:

1. Flatten a slab of clay with the palm of your hand. Press a margarine or coffee can lid onto the slab to make a circular impression. This will serve as a round base for the pot. Cut out the base.

2. To form the sides of the pot, roll several pieces of clay between the palms of your hands, making a smooth rope of clay about ½" (1.3 cm) to 1" (2.5 cm) thick. Coil a clay "rope" around the outside edge of the pot base.

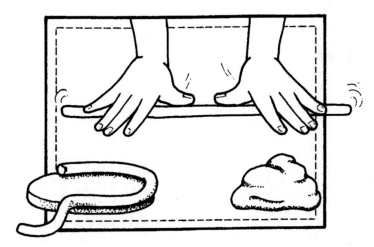

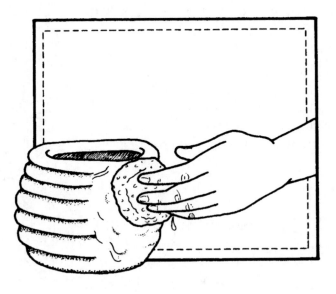

3. Build the sides of the pot by adding more clay coils on top of the first row. If a new piece of clay rope must be attached to finish a row, pinch the rope ends together and smooth the connected section with a moist sponge. When all the rows are finished, apply a moist sponge with gentle fingertip pressure to smooth the entire surface.

4. If desired, use a craft stick, or a plastic fork or knife to create designs in the surface of the pot. Allow the pot to dry before handling.

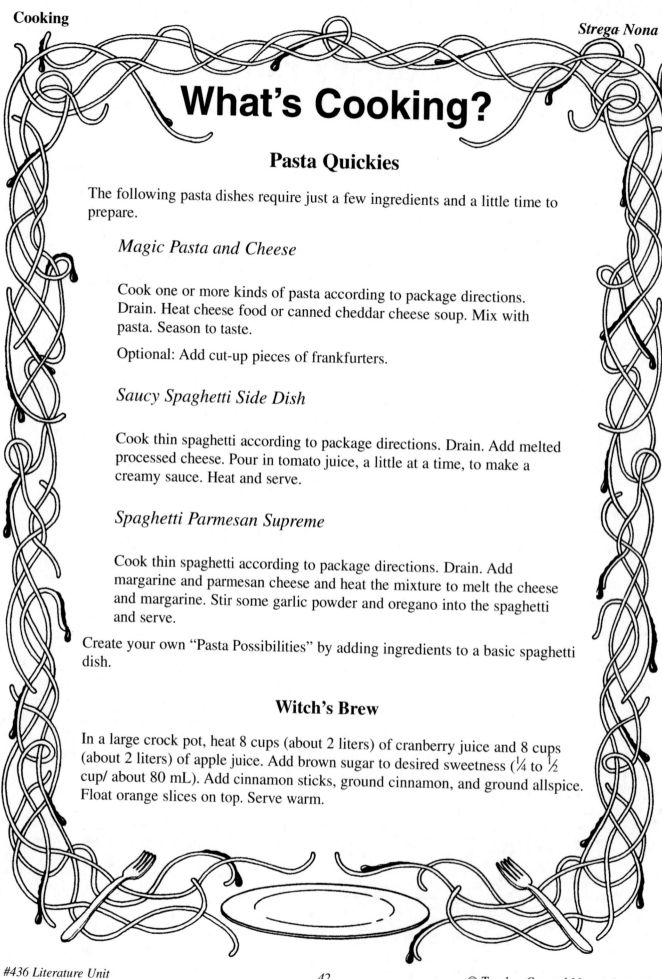

What's Cooking?

Pasta Quickies

The following pasta dishes require just a few ingredients and a little time to prepare.

Magic Pasta and Cheese

Cook one or more kinds of pasta according to package directions. Drain. Heat cheese food or canned cheddar cheese soup. Mix with pasta. Season to taste.

Optional: Add cut-up pieces of frankfurters.

Saucy Spaghetti Side Dish

Cook thin spaghetti according to package directions. Drain. Add melted processed cheese. Pour in tomato juice, a little at a time, to make a creamy sauce. Heat and serve.

Spaghetti Parmesan Supreme

Cook thin spaghetti according to package directions. Drain. Add margarine and parmesan cheese and heat the mixture to melt the cheese and margarine. Stir some garlic powder and oregano into the spaghetti and serve.

Create your own "Pasta Possibilities" by adding ingredients to a basic spaghetti dish.

Witch's Brew

In a large crock pot, heat 8 cups (about 2 liters) of cranberry juice and 8 cups (about 2 liters) of apple juice. Add brown sugar to desired sweetness ($\frac{1}{4}$ to $\frac{1}{2}$ cup/ about 80 mL). Add cinnamon sticks, ground cinnamon, and ground allspice. Float orange slices on top. Serve warm.

"Strega Nona and Big Anthony"

©1992 Mary Ellen Hicks (used by permission)

"Strega Nona and Big Anthony" *(cont.)*

by Mary Ellen Hicks

Verse 1

Strega Nona was a woman,
A witch, of some renown.
Magic cures and secret potions,
Sent whispers through her town.
But she was old and weary,

So on a sign wrote down,
"I need someone to fetch the water.
My garden's turning brown,
My garden's turning brown."

Verse 2

Big Anthony, who never listened,
Was hired then that day.
For following Strega Nona's orders
He'd have a place to stay.

One warning to Anthony,
With these words she did say,
"My pasta pot is very costly,
So keep your hands away,
So keep your hands away!

Verse 3

Anthony, he was so foolish,
On Strega Nona did spy.
He saw the pasta boil and bubble,
And to his neighbors did cry.
"How wicked Big Anthony,

To tell us such a lie!"
Said Anthony, "I'll make the pot cook,
If she can, so can I,
If she can, so can I!"

Verse 4

One day when Strega Nona left,
He put the pot on the floor.
He spoke the magic words
And asked his friends,
"Who wants some more?"

Everyone had plates full,
And some had three or four.
But when the magic would not stop,
The pasta poured out the door,
The pasta poured out the door.

Verse 5

Strega Nona saw the flood
Of pasta as it grew.
She sang the magic tune,
And with it three magic kisses blew.
Then turning to Anthony,

"Your punishment is due,
You'll eat enough to last a lifetime
Before this day is through,
Before this day is through!"

Verse 6

This tale is full of lessons true
That you'll not want to miss.
Obey the rules, and do not brag
To have a life of bliss.

Though I know well these morals,
My favorite one is this:
In spite of all the lovely words,
The magic's in the kiss,
The magic's in the kiss.

Reader's Theater

Reader's Theater is an exiting and easy method of providing students with the opportunity to perform a mini-play while minimizing the use of props, sets, costumes, or memorization. Students read the dialogue of the characters, narrator, chorus, etc., from a book or prepared script. The dialogue may be read verbatim from the book just as the author has written it, or an elaboration may be written by the performing students. Sound effects and dramatic voices can make these much like radio plays.

For *Strega Nona*, you may wish to type out the text from the book in play form, assigning several narrator parts. These typed scripts may be duplicated for the performers and in this way, *Strega Nona* can be easily performed as a play. If you wish to make the following script more like *Strega Nona*, the characters' names can be changed back and the actual chants from the book can be used.

Announcer: Welcome to our Reader's Theater adaptation of the old tale, *Strega Nona,* retold by Tomie dePaola. Our readers are as follows:

Characters:

Announcer	Narrator 3	Sister of the Convent
Narrator 1	Granniwich	Townsperson
Narrator 2	Dominic the Dreamer	Mayor

Townspeople (remainder of the class)

(Note: Children walk "on stage" as they are introduced and stand in the correct order.)

Narrator 1: A long time ago in a little village in Italy there lived a young man named Dominic. Everyone called him Dominic the Dreamer because he dreamed of performing great feats of magic.

Narrator 2: Dominic worked for Granniwich, the old woman of the village, who could make magic potions with just the right ingredients and a special chant.

Narrator 3: Dominic the Dreamer always seemed to be getting in trouble with his grand ideas and he was just a little bit lazy. One day he went to ask Granniwich an important question.

Dominic: Granniwich, will you teach me some of your magic spells?

Granniwich: Oh, Dominic, you just aren't ready to learn any magic. You're too young, and I'm afraid you would get everything all mixed up.

Narrator 1: Dominic the Dreamer didn't listen to Granniwich. He started telling all the people in town that he could do magic—like making things disappear or reappear, grow or become very small.

Narrator 2: Unfortunately, no one believed Dominic and they made fun of him.

Narrator 3: Dominic the Dreamer was very upset because all the townspeople were laughing at him.

Dominic: *(to the townspeople)* I don't like the way you have all been laughing at me. I'm going to show you that I really do know how to make magic. I can make this pot cook enough lunch for all of you!
(to himself) Now what was that magic chant I heard Granniwich saying the other day? Let's see
(to the townspeople) Begin your cooking, big black pot,
Make some lunch and make a lot!

Reader's Theater *(cont.)*

Narrator 1: But Dominic could not remember the rest of the chant, and so nothing happened. The townspeople began to talk.

Mayor: Dominic, you don't know any of Granniwich's magic spells.

Sister: Why don't you just give up, Dominic?

Townsperson: Come on. Let's all go home.

Dominic: No! No! Give me another chance. It's right on the tip of my tongue. *(To himself)* I hope this is it!

> Boil and bubble, make a bunch,
> Just enough to give us lunch!

Narrator 2: The townspeople watched the pot for a minute or so and then they began to laugh.

Mayor: Oh, Dominic, when will you ever learn not to brag?

Sister: Granniwich knows better than to teach you any of her magic spells.

Townsperson: We aren't going to listen to you anymore, Dominic.

Narrator 3: They all started to walk away, but Dominic called them back.

Dominic: Wait! I think I remember the magic chant. Listen!

> Begin your cooking big black pot,
> Make some lunch and make a lot!
> Get the forks and spoons and plates,
> Hurry, pot, before it's too late!

Narrator 1: The big black pot started to make lunch. At first, it made spaghetti. Then it began to cook macaroni and cheese!

Narrator 2: They all grabbed some plates, forks, and spoons, and began to eat.

Mayor: Oh, this is simply delicious!

Sister: Look! Now the pot is making noodle soup!

Townsperson: Here come some lasagna noodles! Where's my plate?

Dominic: Hey! This is great! I'm going to be a hero in this town! No one will ever laugh at me again!

Mayor: We think you're wonderful, Dominic. We should never have laughed at you.

Sister: You really are smart, Dominic. Thanks for lunch!

Townsperson: You can stop the pot now, Dominic, we're all full!

Narrator 3: Dominic the Dreamer remembered the magic chant to stop the pot.

Reader's Theater *(cont.)*

Dominic: Lunch, lunch in the pot,
Now you're cooked and steaming hot.
Black pot, you have served us well,
End right now this magic spell.

Narrator 1:   Dominic said the right chant to stop the pot, but the pot kept making all kinds of pasta foods—spaghetti, macaroni and cheese, noodle soup, and lasagna. It wouldn't stop!

Mayor: Oh, Dominic, you never do anything right.

Sister: What are we going to do? We're going to drown in our lunch!

Townsperson: Help! Someone get Granniwich!

Granniwich: Did someone call me? Uh, oh. I can see that Dominic the Dreamer has been causing trouble again. Well, here I am. Granniwich to the rescue, as usual.

Narrator 2:   Granniwich performed her magic actions. She turned around three times and clapped her hands twice. The pot stopped right away.

Granniwich: *(turns around three times and claps her hands twice)* That should do it.

Dominic: Oh, *grazia,* thank you, Granniwich. I promise never to try any of your magic spells again. Please don't be angry with me.

Granniwich: Well, Dominic, I think the first thing we're going to have to do is get rid of all this food. Now let me see. What would be a good way to do that? *(Talking to the audience)* Does anyone have any ideas about how to get rid of all this food? Raise your hand if you have an idea. *(She calls on two or three children who have their hands up.)*

Narrator 3:   *(to the audience)* Thank you for your suggestions. I'm sure Granniwich and the townspeople will know just how to solve the problem now.

Narrator 1:   Yes, Dominic the Dreamer learned his lesson the hard way. He was lucky Granniwich came along just in time.

Announcer: We hope you enjoyed our adaptation of *Strega Nona*. We will now present a poem called "Strega Nona's Magic Pot." Our readers for the poem are _____, _____, _____, and _____ .
(Teacher: You may want to select one student to read each stanza of the poem. See poem on page 17.)

Announcer: We will now sing a song called "Strega Nona and Big Anthony." (Teacher: See song on pages 43 and 44. You may also want to sing "On Top of Spaghetti," referred to an page 10.)

Announcer: This is the end of our program. Thank you for being such good listeners.

Bibliography

Related Literature

Aardema, Verna. *Why Mosquitoes Buzz in People's Ears: A West African Tale.* (Dial, 1975)

Barrett, Judi. *Cloudy with a Chance of Meatballs.* (Macmillan Child Group, 1982)

Comanska, Janina. *Marek, the Little Fool.* (Greenwillow, 1982)

Frascino, Edward. *Nanny Noony and the Magic Spell.* (Pippin, 1988)

Galdone, Paul. *The Magic Porridge Pot.* (Houghton Mifflin Co., 1979)

Himmelman, John. *Amanda and the Magic Garden.* (Viking, 1987)

Peet, Bill. *Whingdingdilly.* (Houghton Mifflin Co., 1982)

Prelutsky, Jack. "The Spaghetti Nut," from *Sing a Song of Popcorn.* (Scholastic, 1988)

Silverstein, Shel. "Spaghetti," from *Where the Sidewalk Ends.* (Harper Collins Child Books, 1974)

Westwood, Jennifer. *Going to Squintum's: A Foxy Folktale.* (Harcourt Brace Jovanovich, 1985)

Other Books by Tomie de Paola *(partial list)*

The Legend of the Indian Paintbrush. (Putnam Pub Group, 1988)

Little Grunt & the Big Egg: A Prehistoric Fairy Tale. (Holiday, 1990)

The Mysterious Giant of Barletta: An Italian Folktale. (Harcourt Brace Jovanovich, 1988)

Nana Upstairs & Nana Downstairs. (Puffin Books, 1978)

Now One Foot, Now the Other. ((Putnam Pub Group, 1992)

Pancakes for Breakfast. (Harcourt Brace Jovanovich, 1987)

Sing, Pierrot, Sing. (Voyager Books, 1987)

The Talking Coat. (PH Enterprises, 1987)

Tony's Bread. (Putnam Group, 1989)

Too Many Hopkins. (Putnam Pub Group, 1989)

The Quicksand Book. (Holiday, 1977)

Join Us as We Present Our Reader's Theater Adaptation of *Strega Nona*

Date: _____   **Time:** _____

Place: _____

Presented by _____